My Secret Life as Peanut

Wild Icon Publishing Group – Fort Lauderdale, FL

2009

My Secret Life as Peanut

Todd Friedman

&

Megan Andrews

Copyright © 2009 by Todd Friedman
2nd Edition

All rights reserved.
No part of this book may be used or reproduced in any manner whatsoever without written permission.

All photos were taken by Todd Friedman.
No photos were staged.
They were captured as best as possible,
as they happened.

Published in the United States by
Wild Icon Publishing Group.
www.WildIcon.com
info@wildicon.com

First edition previously cataloged as follows:

Library of Congress Cataloging-in-Publication Data
Friedman, Todd.
My secret life as Peanut / Todd Friedman, Megan Andrews. -- 1st ed.
p. cm.

SUMMARY:
This animal tale about a lovable mischievous cat, and her secret life next door is based on a real pet, Sassy, also known as Peanut. The story includes facts about cats, in a chapter book format, suitable for early readers.
LCCN 2008924968
ISBN-13: 978-0-9799335-3-0
ISBN-10: 0-9799335-3-6

1. Cats--United States--Anecdotes.   I. Andrews, Megan II. Title.

SF445.5.F75 2008   636.8

Printed and bound in the U.S.A.

This book is dedicated to our special friend, Peanut, and the millions of animals who need loving homes.

Giving Back

Thanks for buying my book! Your support allows me to help other animals who need homes. I partner with and donate a portion of book sales to selected organizations whose goals are to care for and place animals in homes. These organizations made it possible for me and my siblings to be adopted and have a loving home.

Table of Contents

Chapter 1: About Me 1

Chapter 2: What Happened 3

Chapter 3: Moving Day 6

Chapter 4: The Animal Place 9

Chapter 5: My New Home 13

Chapter 6: Turtles and Rabbits 16

Chapter 7: The Jones 18

Chapter 8: Getting Settled 20

Chapter 9: I Meet the Neighbors 24

Chapter 10: The Hills 28

Chapter 11: I Become Peanut 31

Chapter 12: My New Playground 34

Chapter 13: A Lazy Summer Day 38

Chapter 14: The Rabbits' Invasion 40

Chapter 15: Lap Cat 44

Chapter 16: Raining Cats and Dogs 48

Table of Contents

Chapter 17: Bad Kitty..52

Chapter 18: My Potty Place................................55

Chapter 19: A Special Cushion for Me.................58

Chapter 20: Life of the Party...............................60

Chapter 21: My Christmas Ornament 63

Chapter 22: The Runaway Catnip Toy 65

Chapter 23: My Necklace.....................................69

Chapter 24: The Curious Calico 72

Chapter 25: A Very Good Year 74

Acknowledgements

Our most sincere thanks to:

- Our parents for their encouragement and for ensuring we had the invaluable experience of owning and enjoying pets throughout our childhoods.

- Our neighbors for sharing their pet with us. They are a wonderful family and good people.

- Maria Sanchez, a friend who inspired us to share this priceless story. (She sent Peanut the engraved gold necklace featured in the book).

- Our young second cousin, Payton Weinzapfel, who read the book in its early stages and provided invaluable advice.

- People who told us there are already thousands of books published about animals. We love a challenge!

- The writers' support group in Dallas for its encouragement and advice.

- Our amazing and impressive graphic designer, Lisette Richter (L2 Design), for her dedication to the book cover design and other needs.

- Our editor, Debbie Copening, for reading it to her second grade class and offering sound advice and editorial support.

~ Introduction ~

"My Secret Life as Peanut" is a touching true story with genuine photos. It is a delightfully entertaining, funny and educational story that adults will love as much, if not more, than children.

The captivating story, told through the eyes of an animal, is about a lovable and mischievous cat with a secret life at the neighbors. It tells about the evolution of their relationship and how she maintains a secret life next door. She also educates readers about cats, providing interesting cat facts throughout the story.

This story is priceless. We hope you enjoy her story as much as we have enjoyed sharing it with you.

~ Chapter 1 ~

About Me

Hi, my name is Sassy. I am a calico cat and I want to tell you my story. I think you will like it!

I am a typical calico cat with lots of pretty colors. I have patches of black, brown and orange fur. My paws and belly are white as snow.

I have big, green eyes and a pink nose. Beneath my pink nose, I have brown fur in the shape of a moustache. And, I have really long whiskers. Cat whiskers are supposed to be like your fingertips. They help me sense the presence, size and shape of nearby objects.

I am also smaller than most calico cats. I think I could have been a runt. Runts are the smallest in the litter. They are special because each litter has only one runt.

My Fun Cat Facts

Most of my fellow calico cats are girls, just like me. Something called genes gives us our color. The same genes that give us our three colors also make us girls. Sometimes, but not often, a boy calico is born. He will usually only have one or two colors.

Also, did you know that all cats have 24 whiskers? We have four rows of whiskers on each side. I can move the top rows of my whiskers without moving the bottom ones. We are talented creatures!

~ Chapter 2 ~
What Happened?

In my first home, I was an only pet. My owners were Mr. and Mrs. Higby. They were a young couple who had no children. They provided a loving home and gave me lots of attention.

I had a nice life. I played and took naps while the Higbys worked all day. At night, we all watched TV together after dinner. I loved to curl up next to them. They always gave me lots of love.

One night, Mr. Higby gave me my dinner. He always fed me before they sat down to their dinner. He and Mrs. Higby began talking. Well, mostly Mr. Higby talked and she listened. Then, Mrs. Higby sighed and shook her head. I think they were sad.

Mrs. Higby reached down and picked me up and said, "Oh Sassy, I don't want to move, but sometimes adults have to make hard decisions. What are we going to do?"

What? She's asking me? How am I supposed to know? I just meowed and licked her cheek. I didn't care where we lived. The most important thing was being together.

My Fun Cat Facts

I have the largest eyes of any mammal in relation to my body size. Look at my picture and you'll see what I mean. Each of my eyes is bigger than my little mouth. I think you would probably look funny if your eyes were that big.

Also, I can see about six times better than you when it's a little bit dark out. At night, my eyes can scoop up even the smallest bit of light. That is why we cats are such good hunters at night.

We don't see a lot of detail, though. We are really good at seeing movement. Have you ever seen a cat quickly jump at a mouse or bug? The slightest movement never goes unnoticed by us.

~ Chapter 3 ~
Moving Day

Soon, I noticed boxes everywhere. I guess the Higbys decided we had to move. I was excited. I had never lived anywhere else.

Maybe our new house will be taller. Maybe it will have those stairs I see in the TV houses. Oh, and maybe it will have a big backyard. I can't wait! Just think about the new opportunities! Even though I am excited, I think I will miss our home.

One morning, a big truck parked in front of our house. I was climbing all over the boxes. It was like having a big fort! Soon, strangers put all the boxes in the truck. My fort quickly disappeared. I got scared. I was afraid they'd put me in the big, noisy truck.

I couldn't find anywhere to hide. All the furniture was gone. The only place to go was outside. I ran out the front door. Mr. Higby shouted, "Sassy, come back here!"

I stared at him from the sidewalk. He was holding my kitty carrier. I hate my carrier. It always means I have to go get shots. But wait. I bet we are going to our new house. It had to be!

I slowly walked back to the front door. I let Mr. Higby put me in the carrier. We all got in the car.

We drove away from the house. Mrs. Higby was crying. Mr. Higby seemed grumpy. I wish they could be excited like me. I chirped out a few happy meows.

Soon, the car stopped at a small building. Mrs. Higby took me out of my carrier. She held me tight. Tears were streaming down her cheeks. She said, "Good-bye, Sassy. I will miss you so much." She kissed the top of my head. Then she placed me back into the carrier.

What? Good-bye? Why is she telling me good-bye? What is going on? I thought we were all moving together. We were a family.

My Fun Cat Facts

Did you know that cats can make 100 different sounds? We don't just meow. We can make chattering sounds when we see birds, purring when we are happy, and lots of other funny sounds, even like chirping.

~ Chapter 4 ~
The Animal Place

Mr. Higby carried me into the building. I looked around and saw many other animals in cages. An old man appeared. His hair was white and puffy, just like cotton. I heard Mr. Higby whispering to him. I think I heard him say, "Please find her a good family."

Mr. Higby handed the man the carrier and left. I screamed loud, unhappy meows. I said, "Why are you leaving me? We're a family. I want to come with you!"

He didn't come back. The cotton-haired man put me in a small cage. I was so sad, and I missed my family. They were good to me. I loved them very much. I kept wondering what I did wrong. I didn't understand why they left me behind.

I saw other animals looking at me. I just looked down at my paws. I was afraid I'd cry. I wondered if all their families had also moved.

Finally, a funny looking dog with curly hair said, "My family had to move, too. Don't worry. You did nothing wrong. Sometimes adults move to new places and just can't take pets." I sadly licked my paw and looked away. I didn't feel like talking to him. But I did feel a tiny bit better. I hoped he was right.

The cotton-haired man put a sign above my cage. It said, "My name is Sassy. I'm looking for a nice home." Sometimes, people would stop and look in at me. Most of the time, they just walked away.

One special day, a boy put his face against my cage. He said, "Pssst." He wanted to pet me. I put my nose against the cage. He poked it and smiled. He seemed interested in … me.

Next, a little girl peeked in and smiled. She said, "Oh Mommy, look, I like her. She's so pretty." The mother said, "Mike, you know I always wanted a calico."
I looked at them all and meowed "pick me."

Could it be? Could this possibly be my new family? Just then, the cotton-haired man opened the cage. He picked me up and handed me to the little girl. She pressed her nose against mine. I gave her a few purrs. I remembered the Higbys loved that.

The mother looked at the man and said, "We'll take her." The little girl buried her face in my belly.

Yippee! I had just been adopted.

~ Chapter 5 ~
My New Home

My new family is called the Jones. They put me in their car and we drove off. After a short time, we arrived at a beautiful, tall two-story house. I couldn't wait to get inside. I kept meowing "Hurry up, hurry up, take me inside!"

We got inside, finally. Guess what? My new house had those stairs I wanted. And, it gets even better. A big yellow dog and two cats were waiting for me.

Oh boy, I'm going to have siblings! I always wanted brothers or sisters. All my wishes were coming true. Mrs. Jones put me down. At last, free in my new home!

I ran and ran all around. They chased me, but I was too fast for them. The yellow dog barked. I ran upstairs, then back downstairs. I crawled under tables. I jumped on chairs and beds.

Then I spotted a small door in the kitchen. I went through the door. On the other side was a beautiful, big backyard. Remember, that's the other thing I wished for in a new home.

The backyard had bright green grass. A swimming pool sparkled in the sun. I ran as fast as I could across the grass. Suddenly, I stumbled on something hard.

Ouch! I landed on my back.

My Fun Cat Facts

I can jump five times as high as I am tall. Here's what that would be like for you. If you had five friends lay down in a long straight line, could you jump over them? Probably not!

I slowly rolled over and pushed myself up. But I kept my belly low to the ground. I started backing up onto the sidewalk. Then I sat up and turned my head. I peered across the grass. I was a little bit afraid. I heard the grass rustling. Something was there.

~ Chapter 6 ~
Turtles and Rabbits

A turtle stretched his neck above the grass. A turtle? I blinked a couple times. I wanted to make sure I wasn't seeing things. He looked at me with lazy eyes. I thought he would fall asleep right on the spot! He just stared at me. He must not be afraid of me. He didn't even move. Soon, he returned to eating grass.

I heard some other noises. I turned around and bumped into a cage. I looked in and saw two bunny rabbits. They had really long whiskers, just like me. Their big floppy ears almost touched the ground. One was white with some brown patches. The other one was black. I've never seen real turtles or rabbits—just the ones on TV.

I batted at the cage with my paw. They both looked at me with round, almost black eyes. The black one hopped forward. He sniffed me. His nose was twitching. It looked funny.

Even though it would be fun to stay and play, I wanted to keep exploring. I figured I'd save some excitement for later. I meowed at the rabbits to say I'd be back.

I wanted to clean up before I went inside. So, I licked my paws and rubbed them against my face. This clean-up activity, called grooming, is my way of taking a bath. Once I was done, I ran back inside.

My Fun Cat Facts

Did you know that I spend almost 30% of my life grooming? That is why you see me doing this so often. Also, I lose almost as much saliva when grooming as I do when I go pee pee. So, I have to drink lots of water.

~ Chapter 7 ~

The Jones

Now I'll tell you about the Jones family. Mr. Jones' name is Mike. He is a police officer in town. Mike is tall and has a moustache, just like me. His wife, Susan, is a school teacher. Susan is very pretty and has silky, curly hair. I like her soft, calming voice.

They have two children, Billy and Amy. Billy is 17 and wants to be a doctor. He plays the tuba in the school band and has his own car. Amy is 13. She is on the swim team and is trying out to be a cheerleader.

The other cats are Leo and Felix. Leo is much bigger than me. I think he eats too much because he's a little fat. Felix is solid black and seems shy. The big yellow dog is Toby. Just as I began to wonder if they were

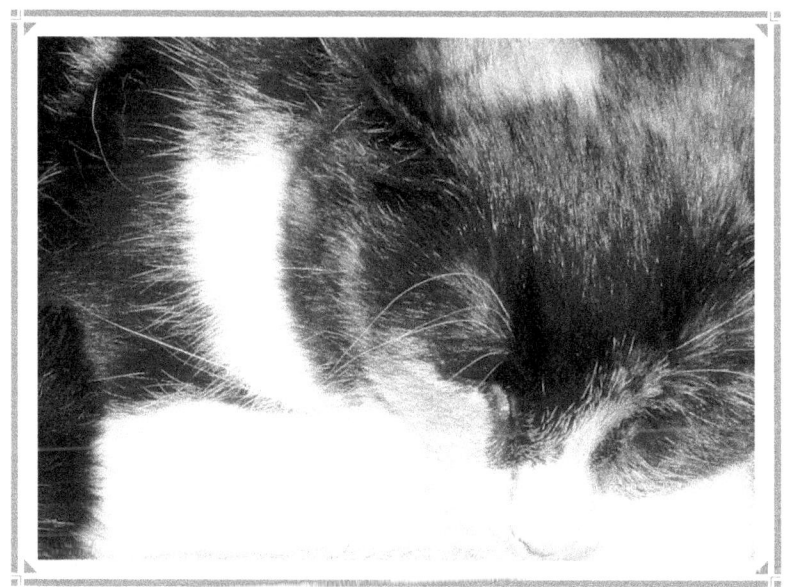

adopted like me, my eyes got very heavy. I let out a big yawn. All the excitement made me want a nap.

I saw a kitty bed in the corner. Mrs. Jones patted it and said, "Sassy, come here and rest." I laid down and fell asleep instantly.

My Fun Cat Facts

Cats sleep about 16 hours a day. That is why we take so many cat naps throughout the day!

~ Chapter 8 ~
Getting Settled

When I first got to the Jones' house, I was a little shy. I had to get used to my new home. Change is hard for cats like me. It takes time for us to feel like we belong.

I think you understand. It's like the first day of school. There are lots of new people. You have to make new friends and figure out where everything is. Once you do that, it's okay. The Jones knew I'd be a bit scared. They made sure I was comfortable and were patient with me.

Leo and Felix told me that all the animals in our family were adopted, just like me. We're all very lucky. I think about all the animals at that place the Higbys left me at. I wondered about the curly haired dog and hoped he found a new family.

Every day brings new surprises—like Toby. At first, I thought I'd be afraid of him. He is big and has a loud bark. But Toby turned out to be like a big teddy bear. He likes to protect me. He always makes sure the other animals are nice to me.

Leo is white with patches of butterscotch. He has a big belly. But I don't call him fat. That's not very nice.

One morning, I woke up late. I felt someone staring at me. I stretched and turned over. Leo was glaring at me! It was kind of scary. He jumped toward me. I was too quick for him. I ran to the side. Leo quickly licked his paws. Then he ran off fast! I could tell he was embarrassed. I beat Leo at his own little game!

Leo loves to play this game. He likes to try and scare me. I think he likes that I don't get scared. That's what makes it fun for him. I'm a challenge.

Leo is just being a cat. Cats are born with a desire to hunt and chase. It's just the way we are. We get bored if it's too easy to catch something.

I have to tell you about my mouse chase. Yesterday, I was napping on the Jones' front porch. I heard the bushes rustling. Then I saw it. A tiny mouse jumped out of the bushes. He saw me and started running. I jumped up and chased him. He ran underneath the car. Then he hopped onto the neighbor's lawn. I pounced on top of him! He fell over, under my belly.

I can't pick things up with my paws like you do. So I put the mouse in my mouth and dropped him at the Jones' front door. This is my way of giving a gift to my family. It's like that time Amy brought her mom a picture that she painted at school.

My Fun Cat Facts

By nature, us cats are explorers. We are always on the hunt for food and things to play with. But don't worry about us too much. We are good explorers because we know to escape danger. That is why people say we have nine lives.

~ Chapter 9 ~
I Meet the Neighbors

This morning I woke up and heard Billy playing the tuba. Amy had something called a "sleepover" last night. All the girls were giggling and being loud.

I went downstairs and the doorbell rang. As usual, Toby started barking. He always barks when the doorbell rings. All these noises upset me. When Mrs. Jones opened the front door, I ran outside.

I usually just sit on the Jones' porch since I'm afraid of the street. This time, I wanted to explore. There's the backyard, but I didn't feel like going there today. The turtle and rabbits were there.

I just wanted to have some peace and quiet!

I decided to go to the neighbors' house. I often see Mr. and Mrs. Jones talking to them. They are friends. Sometime the Jones even go over to their house. I don't know if they have pets or even like cats. I wanted to learn more about my new family's friends.

I walked down the sidewalk to their house. I was a bit curious. Just then, the neighbors' front door opened.

The man walked outside toward the mailbox. I ran down the sidewalk to greet him.

"Hi Sassy," he said. "Aren't you cute?" He started stroking my head. He pet me down my back, up to the tip of my tail. Hee hee. That tickles. I dropped onto my side. He was very nice to me.

I began to roll around on the pavement. I rolled back and forth and back and forth. The man laughed and rubbed my little white belly. I licked his hand. That is my way of giving a kiss.

I heard their door open again. This time, the lady came outside. "Hey Kelly," the man said. "We have a little visitor." She walked over to us. She bent down and pet my head. "Look Kevin," she said, "Sassy is flopping." They looked down at me and smiled.

This marked the beginning of my new friendship with Kevin and Kelly. I now go to the Hills' front yard frequently. I flop on the sidewalk when they are outside. And, I sit on their windowsills when they are inside.

My Fun Cat Facts

When I flop on my back, it means I love and trust you. My belly is the most tender part of my body. I only show my belly to people I know love me and won't hurt me.

~ Chapter 10 ~
The Hills

Before I go much further, I should tell you more about the Hills. Kevin is the husband. His office is at home. Lots of times he has to go meet people at their offices. I think I've heard the Jones call him a salesman.

It's easy for me to know when Kevin is home. I crawl under the bushes and hop up onto the windowsill. I like to meow until he sees me.

Kelly is his wife. She works for a big computer company. Lots of times, I see her with a suitcase. When I see that, I know she will be gone for awhile. I don't like those days. It reminds me of the day the Higbys left me at that place. I can tell Kevin doesn't like it either. He is sad when she goes away.

I think the Hills like me. They come outside to pet me whenever they see me. They talk to me a lot, too.

Kevin told me he wished they could have pets but Kelly is gone too much.

Kelly said she used to have cats when she was growing up. She called them Siamese cats. She said they were very pretty, but they needed lots of attention.

Kevin said when he was a little boy his neighbors had miniature ponies, monkeys, exotic birds, large land tortoises and lots of other animals. He said it was like a zoo right next door!

Wow, can you believe that?

My Fun Cat Facts

In the animal kingdom, I am smarter than everyone else except monkeys. Sometimes I think I may be smarter than humans. But the scientists can't prove that.

~ Chapter 11 ~
I Become Peanut

One evening, I was napping in the Jones' backyard. I heard music drifting from the Hills' house. Kevin and Kelly were outside in their backyard. I could hear them talking. I decided to climb the fence.

The fence was very high. I knew I'd need to get some speed to jump that high. I ran and took a big leap. I also used my claws to help me get to the top. Jumping down was much easier. The grass cushioned my paws when I landed.

Oh my, what a backyard! It has a very beautiful deck with lots of chairs and tables. They even had a little fireplace. Music was playing softly.

The Hills were sitting on the patio. They saw me. Kevin patted the chair next to him. "Come here, Sassy. Let me pet you." I jumped up on the chair. He began to pet me. I started purring.

As I began slipping into a cat nap, I heard Kevin say, "Kelly, do you think she looks like a Sassy?" Kelly was silent for a bit. Then she said, "I'm not really sure."

She stared at me for awhile. Then she said, "Kevin, remember Peanut, our friend's cat? Sassy actually looks like Peanut, but with more brown." Kevin looked at me closely. "Wow, you're right!" he exclaimed. "And since she's so small, it's a perfect name for her."

So Peanut it was! To be honest with you, I like it. It is a fun name. I'm going to make it my secret. I know secrets can sometimes be bad. But this is a good secret.

When I am at the Hills' house, I become Peanut.

Then when I return home, I am back to being Sassy.

I enjoy visiting my new best friends, Kevin and Kelly.

I am a very thankful cat. I now have a loving family and wonderful new friends.

~ Chapter 12 ~
My New Playground

Visiting the Hills in the backyard is one of my favorite things to do. The Hills are usually outside in the morning and at night. Sometimes I take cat naps on the fence and wait for them to come outside.

Other times, I hear the soft music playing. Then I know they are there. Cats have really good hearing. Our hearing is much better than humans or dogs.

Being at the Hills is like a vacation for me. It is always quiet and peaceful. And, I have to tell you about the big wood deck. It is the best thing in the world!

The deck is enormous. It has lots of room for me to crawl beneath it.

My Fun Cat Facts

I love high places. I always like to watch over my house. Us cats are very territorial. That means we like to keep an eye on our area. It's sort of like at school, how some kids hang out in the same place all the time.

Sometimes I find little mice I can chase. I crawl underneath the deck and quietly listen for sounds. When I hear something, I pounce on it!

The deck also has benches to climb on. I love to play on the benches.

Sometimes I also sit on the hot tub cover. After it rains, I like to drink the water that sits on top of the hot tub cover. I know it's probably dirty, but I don't mind. Drinking dirty water is what cats do! Sometimes I even like water that is in a flower vase or the toilet.

My Fun Cat Facts

Let me tell you why we like dirty water! Cats have a very good sense of smell. We can smell things like chemicals and chlorine that are in regular faucet water. Also, you've probably washed our drinking dish with detergent. We can smell that, too.

Therefore, water in puddles, aquariums and flower vases seem much better to us! You should always wash and rinse all detergent from our water and food dishes. Let water from the faucet stand for a while before putting it out for us. Then we won't be so picky.

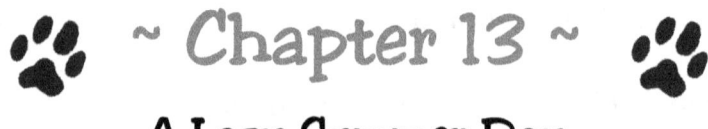

A Lazy Summer Day

It's late summer and very hot. Today, I was curled up in the Jones' backyard. I was feeling sleepy. I was even too tired to climb the fence and go to the Hills.

Mrs. Jones opened the back door and let Toby outside. He walked across the patio and lapped up water from his bowl. Mrs. Jones went to go check on the rabbits. Toby finished drinking and sat down. He sniffed the air, yawned, and laid down. Soon, Toby's eyes got heavy and he was fast asleep. I started to doze off myself.

Suddenly, I heard Mrs. Jones scream. Startled, Toby woke up. He ran over to Mrs. Jones to protect her. He thought she was in danger. I followed. We saw her looking at the rabbits' cage. It was empty! She started running all over the backyard looking for them.

Toby began sniffing around. Just like me, he has an amazing sense of smell. He could smell a dog biscuit miles away. I saw him bury his nose in the grass along the fence. Once Toby finds something, he won't give up.

Mrs. Jones walked over. "Toby, what have you found?" She peered down at him. Toby started pawing at the ground. He looked up at her. Her hand flew to her mouth. She gasped, "Oh, look at that hole, Toby. The rabbits escaped and dug their way next door."

My Fun Cat Facts

Cats have a special scent organ in the roof of our mouths. It figures out smells. That's why you sometimes see us "sneer."

~ Chapter 14 ~

The Rabbits' Invasion

Wait, I thought. The Hills' backyard belonged to me! How dare those rabbits come onto MY territory. I jumped up on the fence to see if I could see them.

Mrs. Jones went next door. She knocked on the front door. Kevin answered. They went to the backyard. I watched them. Mrs. Jones got on her hands and knees.

She peered under the deck. She called out to the rabbits. They would not cooperate. They were being naughty. It was funny to watch. I just stayed on the fence.

I could hear the rabbits scampering around under the deck. They wouldn't listen to Mrs. Jones. The more she called, the further away they hopped. They liked being under the deck, just like me.

Mrs. Jones was furious. She kept yelling at them. Both she and Kevin were trying to grab them. I heard Kevin say he had an idea. He walked over to the garden hose. He turned the water on.

Rabbits don't like water. Kevin and Mrs. Jones sprayed water down the cracks of the deck. Finally, the rabbits hopped out. They did not enjoy the water shower. They were very upset.

Mrs. Jones scooped them up. She apologized to Kevin and took them home. Ha, I thought. It serves them right!

I jumped down the fence into the Hills' yard. The Hills have some long chairs on the deck they call loungers. I like to lie underneath them. It is my favorite hot day resting spot.

I like these chairs because they provide a lot of shade. I can spend hours laying underneath these chairs. They provide relief from the heat.

The Hills also have a plant I like. It sits on top of a stand. It's just the perfect size for me to sit under. I really like sitting underneath things. It makes me feel safe, which is kind of how I feel when I'm up high.

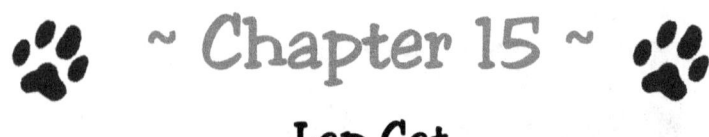

~ Chapter 15 ~
Lap Cat

I wandered to the Hills the next morning. As I jumped up the fence, I thought about yesterday. I was a little selfish about the rabbits. I wanted to have my new friends all to myself. I was afraid they would take away some of the attention I get from the Hills.

I now feel sort of bad for the rabbits. I'm very lucky that I'm allowed freedom. I get to visit the Hills everyday. I'll make sure I play with the rabbits more now. They need friends, too.

Morning is my favorite part of the day. After Kelly wakes up, she makes coffee. The coffeemaker is in the kitchen, near the backyard door. The door has a big window in it so I can see inside.

Like I do on all mornings, I sat on a chair on the Hills' patio. I waited for her to finish making coffee. Then I hopped off my chair and stared into the kitchen at Kelly. I meowed and meowed until she heard me.

Kelly came out and started to pet me. She was in a hurry today, though. I only got to play with her for a few minutes. Then she had to go inside. I guess she had to get ready for work. So Kevin came out a bit later.

He usually gets to play with me longer. I especially like to sit in his lap and rub my face against his hand.

Have you ever heard people call small dogs "lap dogs?" I think it's because they like to sit on people's laps. That must mean I'm a lap cat. I just love to sit on laps!

I often sit on Kevin's lap when he comes outside to play with me. I like to dig my paws into his legs. I don't think Kevin likes this because my claws hurt his legs. Most of the times, he puts a blanket on his lap before I jump up on him. Then my claws don't bother him quite so much.

My Fun Cat Facts

Have you sometimes noticed that cats "knead?" What this means is that we dig our paws into your lap. It's like when you are making cookies or playing with Play-Doh. You mush the dough in your hands and between your fingers. We're not trying to hurt you. This is part of our nature. As kittens, we do this on our mother's belly. When we do this to you, we are remembering our kittenhood.
This usually means we are happy.

~ Chapter 16 ~
Raining Cats and Dogs

A storm rolled into town the next day. It rained "cats and dogs," according to Mrs. Jones. I don't understand what that means. I didn't see any cats or dogs falling from the sky. Sometimes people say strange things. Maybe this was just one of those times.

I hate rain. It spoils my visits to the Hills' house. Usually, I don't leave the Jones' house on rainy days. But today, it didn't start raining until after I was in the Hills' backyard.

The patio gets all wet when it rains. The Hills' patio is not covered. Well, it sort of has a cover called an arbor. The arbor is made up of wood boards in a criss-cross type shape.

But there are cracks between the boards that rain can fall through. So now the patio was getting really wet and cold. I hate when my fur gets wet!

I panicked and looked around. Then I saw the big umbrella on the deck. The umbrella sits over a table. It's really big and it covers the whole table, plus the chairs around it. Usually the umbrella is only open on sunny afternoons.

This time, I was lucky. Kevin forgot to close it. Or, maybe he knew it was going to rain and left it open just for me! I galloped over to the table and hopped onto one of the chairs. I huddled there to stay dry.

You might wonder why Kevin and Kelly don't allow me inside their house. They do love me very much. But they also want to respect that the Jones are my actual owners.

The Jones' house is my true home. Almost every day I visit my friends the Hills. However, I always return home to the Jones family.

Today, I stayed under the umbrella until it stopped raining. After is stopped raining, Kevin and Kelly came outside. They played with me for awhile. I purred and rubbed my face against their legs.

My Fun Cat Facts

Cats are the only animals that purr. We purr when we breath in and out. We don't purr just when we're happy. Sometimes we purr when we are scared. The smart scientist people say we never purr when we are alone. I wonder how they know that?

~ Chapter 17 ~

Bad Kitty

On my next visit to see the Hills, they didn't come out to play with me. I waited and meowed, but the house seemed really quiet. For the next two visits, Kevin and Kelly didn't come outside. I started to worry. Now it was what Mr. Jones calls the weekend, and still no Kevin or Kelly.

Maybe I made them mad. Or, maybe they don't like me anymore. Even worse, maybe they moved just like the Higbys! I was sad. I missed my friends.

I know that sometimes Kelly has to go away for her job. On those days, Kevin plays with me. They never are gone at the same time. I always get love from at least one of them.

I started to get angry. How could they leave me? Why don't they love me anymore? I was very unhappy. I wanted to punish them if they ever came back.

The Hills have a doormat outside the backdoor. I sit on it when I'm waiting for them to come outside. I went over to the doormat. I sat and looked in the window.

For a long time, I just sat there. I began to have mean thoughts. How could I punish them for leaving me?

Then I came up with an idea. I knew exactly what I was going to do! I sort of had to go potty. In fact, I had to go poop. But I didn't want to go home to my litter box.

You will never guess what I did. I went poop on the doormat next to the Hills back door! I knew it wasn't nice, but I was angry.

Later that night, the Hills came home. I was going to hop over the fence into their backyard. But I heard Kevin yell out, "Kelly, come here. Look at what Peanut did while we were gone." I could hear them talking to each other.

Then Kevin started calling my name. I stayed in the Jones' yard. I bet he's going to scold me for being naughty. I stayed there until they went inside. I was a very bad kitty for doing this. That was mean and selfish. The Hills are very good to me. I should be much nicer.

~ Chapter 18 ~
My Potty Place

I told you about my bad potty behavior. So I guess it's okay to tell you something else. I have a "sensitive" issue. It has to do with going potty.

As you know, cats don't use toilets. We cats have litter boxes. We dig holes in the litter to go potty. Then we cover it up. We are very clean and tidy animals. Except when we're being bad and punishing people!

The Hills don't have a litter box. They do have some big planters in the backyard. In warmer weather, they are filled with pretty flowers.

Now it's getting cold. The flowers are drying up. So, Kelly dug them out. But she didn't fill the planters with anything new. She just left the dirt in them.

With no flowers, the planters are like a big litter box. I couldn't resist.

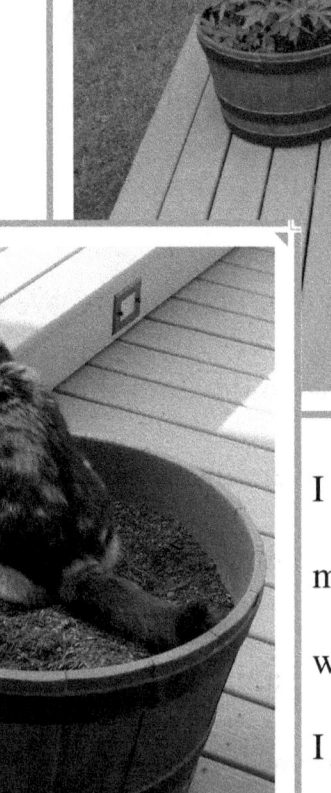

I looked around to make sure no one was watching. I jumped into one of the planters.

I dug and dug, went potty, and covered it up. I got a little bit of dirt on the deck, but maybe the Hills won't notice.

I jumped out of the planter. I ran all over the deck.

I'm not sure why I always feel hyper after going potty.
It's just one of those things.

I jumped on the fence, then onto the roof. I crawled over to the arbor. I have to carefully tiptoe across it or else my tiny paws will fall through the cracks.

Suddenly, I heard Kevin open the door. He must have heard me. I meowed. He looked up at me. Kelly came out after him. I just stared down at both of them like a monkey. This made them laugh.

My Fun Cat Facts

The reason we cover our poop may not be what you think. It can be traced back to cats in the wild. They do this so mean animals won't find and hurt them. Covering our poop is an instinct we are born with. It's an instinct to protect ourselves.

~ Chapter 19 ~
A Special Cushion for Me

Kevin and Kelly went back inside for a moment.

Soon they came back out with soft, plush cushions.

They use these cushions when sitting on the chairs.

These cushions are off limits for me. Since I shed a lot,

I usually get a small towel instead.

On this day, Kevin put a cushion on an empty chair. He patted it and called out to me by my nickname "P-ster." Yippee! I get my own cushion. This really means I'm loved. Maybe they didn't see me use the planter as my potty place. From that day on, I had my own cushion.

I forgot to tell you, the Hills call me some fun names. Sometimes they call me "P-ster," "Super P," or "Sweet P." Sometimes they just simply call me "P."
I like all these nicknames. When I hear any of those names, I know they are calling out to me.

My Fun Cat Facts

We get our sense of security from your voice. Talk to us! Make sure you use the right tone. We know when you're yelling at us. So if we do something bad, we'll know. Sometimes I'll respond better to a lady. Her voice is higher pitched so she sounds nicer.

~ Chapter 20 ~
Life of the Party

Now it's getting colder. Christmas must almost be here. The Jones put up one of those trees. The Higbys used to do that. They would put lots of shiny balls on the tree. I liked to bat at them.

Tonight the Hills are having a big party with lots of people. When the Hills have company, I am usually the

"life of the party." That's what Kelly says because I greet all the guests when they arrive. I love new people. I guess I'm just a curious calico.

I wandered into the Jones' bedroom. Mrs. Jones was curling her hair and Mr. Jones was buttoning his shirt. They must be going to the party.

Maybe this time I shouldn't be at the Hills' front door when the Jones arrive. Mr. Jones tells me I should mind my own business and leave the Hills alone. I decided to go to the Hills' backyard and watch the party from there.

I went outside and hopped over the fence and hid in the bushes. The Hills' yard looked so beautiful. Candles were lit. All the sparkly lights in the trees were turned on. I could see people inside laughing and having fun. I slowly walked across the deck toward the windows to see better. I saw the Jones arrive. I sat and watched for a long time. I wish Kevin and Kelly would come out and play with me. Suddenly, the door opened and Mr. Jones came outside with Kevin. He spotted me.

"Sassy, what are you doing here? I keep telling you not to bother the neighbors." He picked me up and put me on the fence. "Now, jump down. Go home, Sassy."

I heard Kevin say, "That's okay, Mike, we like Sassy. She's not a bother." Kevin winked at me. They went back inside and I stayed in the backyard, out of sight.

My Fun Cat Facts

Did you know that the smart scientists say having cats is good for your health? They can prove that we make your blood pressure lower. This is supposed to be good. It's hard not to feel better when we purr and give you love.

~ Chapter 21 ~
My Christmas Ornament

The next day, I decided to go flopping on the Hills' sidewalk. It was the time of day that Kevin gets the mail. I saw Kelly in the window. She was standing in front of a Christmas tree.

I walked up to the porch and sat in front of the window. I could see Kelly hanging shiny balls and toys on the tree. I just sat there, watching. Kelly must have sensed I was there. She turned around and smiled. She picked something up and came outside.

"Look P-ster, I have an ornament with your photo in it." I looked at it. It was a tiny, flat Santa. It had a small clear window in it.

Wait, that looks like me inside the window. "Yep, that's you Peanut. You have a special place on our tree."

She hung it on the tree, right up front! How funny is that? I ran home and was so happy.

My Fun Cat Facts

Did you know that cats don't like the smell of orange or lemon? Try hanging an orange or lemon scented air freshener on your Christmas tree. Then, we might leave the tree alone!

~ Chapter 22 ~
The Runaway Catnip Toy

The Higbys used to buy me toys for Christmas. But I'm not into toys. I prefer to play with people. Toys don't interest me. The Hills don't know this yet.

Kevin and Kelly bought me a toy with catnip in it. It was a soft black and white mouse. I batted at it to pretend I liked it. Kevin and Kelly thought this was quite funny. I like to make them laugh. I held it between my paws and nibbled on it. After awhile I got bored with the toy and walked away from it.

"Oh come on, Peanut," said Kevin. "Why won't you play with the toy? Here, maybe you'll like this one better." Kevin rolled a plastic toy toward me. It had a bell inside it.

I liked that toy even less than the other one. I don't like toys that make noise. I rubbed my face against his shoe. I'd rather play with Kevin and Kelly. For now, I just left the toys on the patio.

Later, I actually started to like the catnip toy. It was soft and chewy. I decided to take it home with me in my mouth. It was not stealing, since it was a toy given to me, right? I ran home with the toy. I dropped it on the lawn for now. I went inside to take a nap.

After I woke up, I sat in a windowsill upstairs. Kevin and Kelly walked by the house. They stopped, and Kevin pointed at the lawn. I raised my tail and curled it slightly. That always happens when I'm being curious.

I watched, wondering what they were going to do. They looked at each other. Then they looked at the toy.

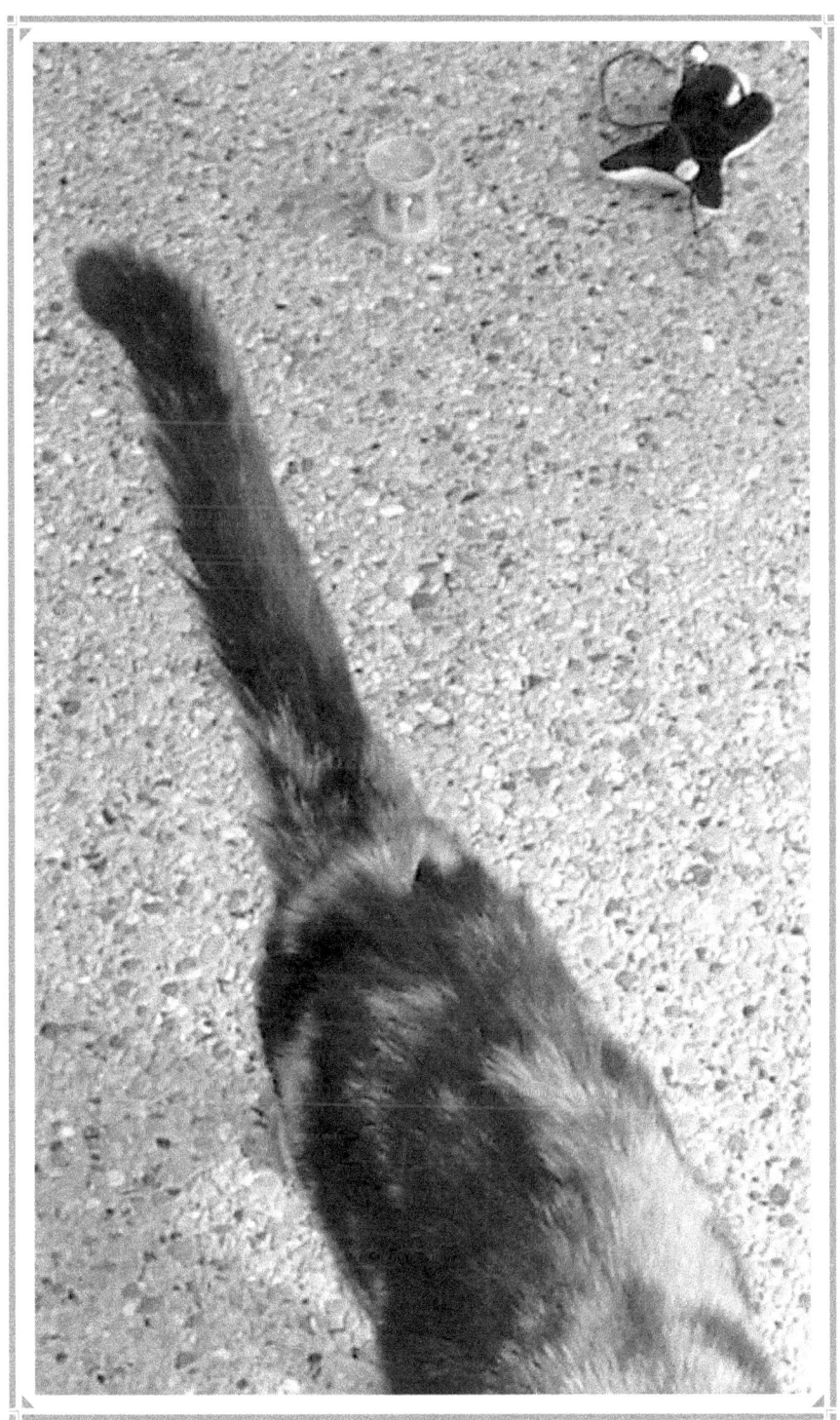

They were laughing. I think they were trying to decide if they should pick up the toy.

Maybe they didn't want the Jones to know they bought me a toy. Mr. Jones did say I shouldn't bother the neighbors. Kevin and Kelly do not want me to lose my outside privileges so they left the toy alone.

Later that day I went to go get my toy. It was gone! I don't know what happened to it. I bet Leo took it and hid it from me. He still likes to be a bully.

My Fun Cat Facts

One of my prettiest features is my tail. My tail is what I use to keep my balance. Did you know I have about 20 bones in my tail? Each of my bones is surrounded by a muscle. That allows me to wag my tail and move it around. Speaking of bones, I have more bones in my body than you do. Cats have 230 bones, and you have 206. Imagine that, for a little animal like me!

My Necklace

I also got some jewelry for Christmas this year. The Hills told one of their friends about my secret life as Peanut. Their friend found it to be very funny.

She sent Kevin and Kelly a gift just for me! It is a very pretty gold necklace in a pink bag. I think I like the pink bag better than the necklace. It's fuzzy and soft.

Kevin and Kelly really like the necklace. It has a gold tag hanging from it. The tag has my nickname, "P-ster." On the other side, it has the Hills' home phone number. Isn't that funny? If I wore that home and the Jones called the number, then my secret would be out!

Luckily, the Hills didn't put the necklace on me. Whew, I hate things around my neck!

For now, the Hills keep the necklace in the pink bag. I saw them put it in a cabinet in the kitchen. Now when I come over to their patio when they have friends over, they bring out the necklace. They like to tell my story to their friends. Everyone laughs and thinks it's very funny that I have this secret life next door.

My Fun Cat Facts

Since I'm friendly, I like lots of the Hills' friends. I even like the ones who say they aren't cat people! Have you ever noticed that cats often walk straight to people who aren't cat lovers? Sometimes people who like cats stare at us and make us nervous. A direct stare is like a challenge for us. Therefore, we may decide to go to the "safest" person in the room, which is the one not looking at us!

~ Chapter 24 ~
The Curious Calico

Remember I said I was a curious calico? Well, I really want to see the inside of the Hills' house. One of their rules is not to let me inside. I think I mentioned that before. They aren't being mean. They want to make sure I know my real home is at the Jones.

A few days after Christmas, it was windy and rainy. Kelly was making her morning coffee. I meowed and meowed. She saw me. She disappeared for awhile. She came back with a jacket on.

As soon as she opened the door, I ran inside. I was so fast I don't think she knew what happened. She called after me. I ran through their family room. I hid behind the couch. She saw me and picked me up.

"Peanut, you know you're not supposed to come inside." She kissed my head and put me back outside. She closed the door.

Kevin came to the kitchen. He must have heard all the noise. I could see them talking. Kevin opened the door to come pet me. I dashed inside once more.

Kelly grabbed me again. They were laughing. She put me back outside. Then she turned to go back into the kitchen. But Kevin still had the door open. So, I went inside a third time. This is a fun game!

Now I think Kelly was mad. She put me outside. When she stood up, she hit her head on the door. Oops! Now I feel kind of bad. But I could still see both of them smiling at me. Maybe they like that I'm a curious calico!

~ Chapter 25 ~
A Very Good Year

It's been a very good year for me. I was adopted by a great family. I have some new best friends, Kevin and Kelly Hill. The Jones give me love, food, shelter, and the stability of a family. The Hills provide friendship, love, and a quiet place when I want to relax.

I have enough love for all of them. And, I love them all for different reasons.

I'm excited for next year. I'm hopeful lots of good things will happen. I have learned that when you love others, you get lots of love back. I guess I am pretty smart.

I understand that you can have both family and friends. They play different roles. One isn't better than the other.

Loving your friends doesn't mean you love your family less. And, loving my family doesn't take away love for friends. I am very lucky to have both!

My Fun Cat Facts

Cats and kittens do best when they have another cat in the family. When possible, we want humans to adopt us together. So adopt two cats or kittens if you can!

About the Authors

The writers are Todd Friedman and Megan Andrews.

Todd and Megan together have founded several companies dedicated to raising funds for animal support charities, veterans, and other not-for-profit organizations.

Thank You For Giving Back With Us!

Nobody can do everything, but everyone can do something.

~ Author Unknown

www.ingramcontent.com/pod-product-compliance
Lightning Source LLC
Chambersburg PA
CBHW071733040426
42446CB00012B/2337